# Kathleen Richardson

# F**K BOY FREE

# FREE

## 10 WAYS TO REPEL F**K BOYS AND ATTRACT THE MAN OF YOUR DREAMS

PRINT ISBN: 978-1-54399-083-6

EBOOK ISBN: 978-1-54399-084-3

# TABLE OF CONTENTS

\* \* \*

*"I've loved another with all my heart and soul, and to me this has always been enough"*

*Nicholas Sparks*

\* \* \*

\* \* \*

*This book is dedicated to my kindred spirit;*
*the man who loves me while I continually learn*
*to love myself more.*

\* \* \*

# INTRODUCTION

*"Pain is something to master, not wallow in."*

*Anais Nin*

I was the bitter baby mama. I wore my hurt, bitterness and anger like a badge of honor. It was cloaked under makeup, designer clothes, degrees, accolades, excess weight and my all-time favorite, religion. I was struggling to navigate the effects of a childhood trauma that left me wounded and in pain. This unhealed pain eventually manifested in the relationships I had with men. I became intensely and intimately involved with f**k boys. They were the hurt that hurt so good. That was until I was just left with the hurt. I've been cheated on and humiliated. I've been physically, emotionally and verbally abused. But I've also laughed until my stomach hurt and felt butterflies. I was supported, cared for, rescued and taken to depths of physical pleasure that left me speechless. While the bad was really bad, the good with these f**k boys was also really good. But I wasn't satisfied with a mix of both good and bad. I wanted only the good in my future relationships. I decided that I was going to manifest the man of my dreams and live the life with him that I imagined. I made the choice to stop recycling the same relationship with different f**k boys. I didn't know if it was possible, but I was determined to find out.

In 2017, I came face to face with my kindred spirit in the Buffalo Airport. I was a nervous wreck waiting for him and I thought I was going to throw up. We had been talking on the phone non-stop for 2 months and I was finally going to meet him in person. When we finally saw each other and hugged, it was at that moment I knew he was IT. Here he was, my wildest hopes and dreams in the flesh. And a fine ass one with muscles at that. And he loved me. All of me. After everything I had been through in my past relationships, I believed I was too damaged to be any man's first choice. What I failed to realize was the power of being healed and whole. My commitment to personal growth and self-healing allowed me to meet a man who chose me.

I transitioned from a man telling me that he would kill me and walk out the door like nothing had ever happened, to a man telling me he wasn't going anywhere, no matter what happens. This would not be possible if I had not done the work outlined in this book. Following the 10 strategies, steps or concepts (whichever you prefer), in this book will begin your journey to becoming f**k boy free and attract the man of your dreams. But first you must find yourself. Your true self that is. The woman hidden and buried underneath the false reality of who you think you are or who you've been told to be. The woman buried beneath the pain and struggles of the past. Once you find yourself, then your kindred spirit will find you. It is my prayer and affirmation that as you read this book you will pull on the self-love and courage that is always present within to radically change your life. It is my prayer and affirmation that you will decide to never stop pursuing your deepest desires. I believe so many of us are afraid to express how much we want to be loved by a man. And there is nothing wrong with that. We were wired to be loved and protected. To deny that is to deny who you are as a woman. This denial causes us to settle for half-ass love from f**k boys. In my opinion, some love ultimately means no love. What we mistake for love is really an attachment and love and attachment are not the same.

Each chapter ends with an exercise that will help bring the concepts to fruition in your life. Although not always easy to implement, the strategies are simple. They are a normal and natural part of being a woman. I was working on implementing the 10 concepts I discuss in this book for 3 years before I met my kindred spirit. Within those three years I dated two men. Each man showed fewer and fewer f**k boy tendencies. This demonstrated that I was on the right path. I knew I was getting closer to meeting the "one". I would encourage you to date, practice the concepts, test them out, learn from your mistakes and learn from the men you date. They are a reflection of you.

Thank you for allowing me to be a part of your journey! Thank you for allowing me to impart into your life! Love and light to you all. Love and light...

* * *

*"You will be someone's best thing"*

*r.h. Sin*

* * *

# WHAT IS A F**K BOY?

Before we begin discussing how to be f**k boy free, it's important to discuss what a f**k boy is. A f**k Boy is a man who may
have one or more of the following qualities at his core:

- Emotional immaturity
- Emotional unavailability
- Irresponsibility
- Lack of direction in life
- Cheats, lies and manipulates
- Physically, sexually, or emotionally abusive
- Non-committal
- Disloyal
- Unreliable
- Undependable
- Financially unstable
- Insecure
- May struggle with various forms of addiction
- Married or involved with multiple women
- Beta male (the opposite of an alpha male)

You may think of other qualities that belong on this list when
you reflect on the men you have dated in the past. This list is
not exhaustive but provides a general list of f**k boy qualities.

It is important to distinguish between a man who is inherently good but is prone to make mistakes (like us), and a f**k boy who ultimately brings more pain than joy to our lives. It is also important to clarify that cheating, or abuse of any sort is not a "mistake"; it may lend to the determination that a man is indeed a f**k boy. This book is not male bashing or a reason to denigrate men. It is important to understand that f**k boys have their own journey to travel and their own karma to grapple with. Just as they choose to be who they are and behave a certain way, women must decide if they will entertain f**k boys. This is not to excuse f**k boy behavior, but to transcend it. The greatest change in our lives will always occur when the focus is inward rather than outward. It is always easier to change ourselves than it is to change others. Now that we have defined what a f**k boy is, let's get to the discussion on how to be f**k boy free!

* * *

*"When you learn to love yourself, your taste in men will change"*

*Unknown*

* * *

# CHAPTER 1

# Release Your Ex

*"Whatever life takes from you, let it go"*

*Don Miguel Ruiz*

If you are still holding space for the men and relationships from your past, it will be very difficult, if not impossible to attract the man of your dreams. You will struggle to create a loving connection with your kindred spirit if you refuse to cut the energetic cords tied to your ex. It is important to release the emotional clutter that lives in your heart. You must uproot the bitterness, anger and resentment you feel towards the men from your past. Simply declaring that you are "over him", doesn't mean that you are. It's been my experience that burying something doesn't mean it died. The man of your dreams cannot find you because there is no space for him in your life and heart. I used to watch the reality show Hoarders from time to time. Each episode chronicles two people who are unable to part with any of their possessions or garbage. The "stuff" they accumulated took over every part of their home. This made it difficult to walk, move around or even find a place to sleep. Because they refused to let anything go, they ran the risk of eviction, the loss of their families, and some of them have even faced jail time. This is an extreme example, but this is what can happen to our hearts and lives when we refuse to release the "stuff" from our past relationships. Despite not having any more room, the hoarders always find space for one more piece of junk, knickknack or pet. When we refuse to release the men and emotions from our past relationships, there will always be room for one more f**k boy. He will find himself right at home with all the other garbage in our heart.

I was such a bitter baby mama. I was so angry that my child's father was living what I thought was the life of his dreams. He had no responsibility when it came to caring for our child and I was going into debt to provide for her. I would occasionally rant and rave about how I had to do everything on my own, with absolutely no help from him. While I decided against taking him to court for child support, I still held it against him and began to hate him. While my feelings were partially justified (maybe more than justified), I eventually asked myself was this mindset productive. What was I gaining from this constant exchange of thoughts and ideas in my head? What was I really accomplishing by holding onto negative energy towards him? I decided that instead of complaining about how I had to do everything, I would adopt an attitude of gratitude. I felt gratitude that my child never went without anything that she needed. I had a village that was completely loyal and supportive. I started to show gratitude for my job, my salary, my car, my family and friends, because I was truly blessed. My daughter was healthy and happy. What he did or didn't do started to become irrelevant. Eventually, I became so filled with gratitude, I even began to show gratitude for him There's no way I can love my daughter and not have a sense of love and respect for the man who provided half her DNA. Sometimes I can't believe what I am saying, especially after everything that he put me through. But there is so much power in releasing and letting go. By releasing my anger and bitterness towards him through gratitude, I was able to remove the negative emotional and energetic space in my heart. This created more than enough room and space for my kindred spirit to enter my life and my heart.

Let him go sis! Your ex-husband, ex-lover, your baby's daddy, the man who broke your heart and abandoned you; the man who left you broken, battered, and lonely. Let your attachment to him go. I know he deserves your hatred, bitterness and anger, but you don't deserve it. It's so heavy, so please take it off. One of the things that prevents us from letting go is knowing that we are justified to feel the way we do. If a man cheats on you and leaves you, you have every right to be angry, depressed, sad, hurt, bitter and resentful! But having the right to feel a certain way does not mean you should entertain that feeling. And the question we must ask ourselves is, do we want to be right, or do we want to be healed? Sometimes you can't have both. R. Braut has said, *"Life becomes easier when you learn to accept an apology you never got"*. This is not to minimize the hurt or pain caused by others or make excuses for their poor actions. But we must decide to either hold on or let go. This may prove to be a difficult decision. Often, we find comfort in our justified bitterness and anger. It soothes us to point out what people did or did not do. We find safety in the chip on our shoulders and we learn to carry the burden of our past relationships. We even try to make it look good with beat faces, slayed outfits and stilettos. Anne Wilson Schaef explains it this way:

*"Our old shit is so precious to us. We tenderly harbor our old resentments and periodically throw them pieces of fresh flesh to keep them alive. We nurture our anger. We don't do any-thing to work through or let it go, we just hang on and nurture it. And we wonder why we feel so stuck and held back in our lives. When we hold onto old shit, it weighs us down. It is as if our feet are stuck in fresh tar. There comes a time when we can see that it doesn't really matter what someone has done to us, our holding on to it is hurting us not them, and if we want to heal, we had best take our old shit and fertilize the flowers"*.

Is your old shit precious to you? Releasing the men from our past means taking personal responsibility for the ways in which we love, care for and respect ourselves. Every relationship we enter is a mirror of the relationship we have with ourselves. In the book, The Four Agreements, author Don Miguel Ruiz discusses a phenomenon I'm very familiar with; self-abuse. He explains:

*"In your whole life nobody has ever abused you more than you have abused yourself. And the limit of your self-abuse is exactly the limit of what you will tolerate from someone else. If someone abuses you a little more than you abuse yourself, you will probably walk away from that person. But if someone abuses you a little less than you abuse yourself you will probably stay in the relationship and tolerate it endlessly".*

Again, this is not to excuse anyone's poor or abusive behavior toward us. This is not to excuse the men who have hurt us, cheated on us, or abandoned us. This is not to shame or guilt the victim. The goal is to empower us to radically create a life where we will attract a man who loves us as deeply as we love ourselves. This is an opportunity to take full responsibility and personal accountability for the role we have played in breaking our own hearts. Being able to understand the role I played in my failed relationships has allowed me to release old lovers. My child's father abused me no more than I abused myself (and I was good at it). He could love me no more than I loved myself. One of the ways I engaged in self-sabotaging behavior was to enter relationships with f**k boys who were immature, disloyal and emotionally unavailable. I struggled with low self-esteem. I was not always loving or kind to myself and I attracted men who were not always loving or kind to me either. Because I was not fiercely loyal to myself, it became easier to accept disloyalty from a man. People treat us how we treat ourselves. People love us the way we love ourselves. When they treat us in a way that is incongruent with how we treat ourselves, we will as Mr. Ruiz says, "walk away from that person". When I began to recognize the role I played in my failed relationships with f**k boys, I stopped blaming them entirely. I let them off the hook for the part I played and released them to sort out their karma.

The moment you release your f**k boy ex is the moment that your kindred spirit will begin to make his way to you. When you begin to clear out and release those old feelings, emotions and energy, it sends a wonderful message to the universe that you are ready for something or someone new and exciting. Arielle Ford, author of The Soulmate Secret explains it perfectly:

*"It's imperative that you create emotional, physical, and psychological space in your life...Nature abhors a vacuum. This means that the faster and more completely we clear out the old, the more rapidly and easily we'll draw in the new".*

It may be easier to release an ex f**k boy who really hurt you than a man you are still secretly in love with. There will always be that one f**k boy who would be the perfect man if only he would get his shit together. Are you still hoping that one day he will come to his senses and you two will live happily ever after? Is there someone who got away and you still stalk their Facebook or Instagram to see how he's doing and who he's doing it with? You must release them as well. And if you can't right now, at least acknowledge your true feelings and send blessings to him. If you can't completely remove him, do not allow him to take up your entire heart space. Reserve a small space for the time being, until you can completely cut the cord. One of my favorite quotes that describes the feeling of being attached to someone that does not belong to you is by Beau Taplin. He says, *"But yes, I would say that you were my favorite of all the nowheres I've been"*. Admittedly, "nowheres" although enjoyable, are fleeting. It is always best to move on.

Your heart space must be clear of emotional and energetic clutter. The attachments to past lovers must be lovingly and gently severed. No man will feel welcome in a heart where other men have made a home. And as my favorite poet Upile Chisala has said, engage in the practice of *"letting go of gone things and saying, that wasn't mine, but mine is on the way"*. Never forget, sometimes things don't work out because they weren't supposed to.

*Exercise to release past lovers: Write a list of the men you are energetically connected to or hold space for in your heart. This will include the men you have resentment and bitterness towards and those you may still be in love with. Write a letter to each man expressing how you feel. Tell him why you are angry and hurt. Tell him how much you hate him for the way he let you down. Tell him why you are still holding on, hoping he will change. Feel free to be as brutally honest as you can. You are not going to mail these letters, and no one is going to see them. Give yourself permission to feel as mad or sad as you need to. After you are done writing these letters, sit for a minute or two to assess how you are feeling. Hopefully you will feel a sense of calm and release. Then, rip up the letters in as many pieces as possible. Take them and either burn them or flush them down the toilet. As you watch the torn letters burn or go down the toilet, I want you to visualize the cord* attaching you to each of your exes, being unplugged from your heart. For example, I have an iron that has a retractable cord. When I push the button, the cord gently disappears into the iron. Envision this same process happening to the energy cords that exist between you and each of the men you wrote a letter to. Take a deep breath, in through your nose and out through your mouth. As you exhale, say **"I thank each of my ex-lovers for the time and energy they have given me. They have served their purpose and they are no longer needed. I forgive myself for holding on longer than I should have and now I lovingly release them".**

* * *

"Don't grieve. Anything you lose comes around in another form"

Rumi

* * *

# CHAPTER 2

# Fully Embrace Your Feminine Essence

*"If you want to experience deep spiritual and sexual fulfillment, you must know your natural sexual essence...and live true to it"*

*David Deida*

\* \* \*

*"A woman's personal power and magnetism grow when she connects with her feminine essence"*

*Rachael Jayne Groover*

The next three chapters are going to delve into how feminine essence, masculine energy, and feminine energy relate to being f\*\*k boy free. There is a fundamental difference in energy and essence. This difference must be grasped to understand the distinct and unique inner workings of feminine essence and feminine energy and its use in becoming f\*\*k boy free.

## What is Essence?

By definition, essence is, "the intrinsic nature or indispensable quality of something that determines its character". Essence is also defined as, "the core nature or most important qualities of a person or thing". An essence is the true nature that a person, place or thing embodies. Essence is the life-force.

## What is Energy?

Energy by definition is "the impetus behind all motion and all activity". Energy is an intangible modifiable force believed to emanate from a person, place or thing. "Energy is a vibe, a feeling, an impression".

For the sake of simplicity, essence is who you are, and energy is how you express who you are. There are two types of energy and two types of essences; masculine and feminine. Most women have a natural feminine essence, and most men have a natural masculine essence. Men and women have different essences that produce a state of opposites. This polarity is necessary for relationships to thrive, especially on a romantic and sexual level. This polarity is not always necessary for friendships between men and women. But if there is to be a sexual and romantic chemistry that will lead to a loving and committed relationship, sexual polarity between masculine and feminine essences must be present. A man with a masculine essence will always be attracted to and choose a woman who has a feminine essence. To learn more about the polarity of masculine and feminine essence, read David Deida's book Dear Lover: A Woman's Guide to Men, Sex, and Love's Deepest Bliss. Remember, essence is the core of who you are. It is the intrinsic nature of your being. The dynamic and indispensable quality of who we are is feminine in nature. We must embrace and learn to bask in our feminine essence. But many women reject their feminine essence and in so doing, reject themselves. Rachael Jayne Groover, author of Powerful and Feminine explains that, *"Although most women's feminine essence is their primary essence, many women energetically cover it up, like an old dusty sheet covering a beautiful piece of antique furniture"*.

When you don't embrace your feminine essence, you will inevitably attract f**k boys. Remember, when it comes to essences, opposites attract. If you deny your feminine essence, you will attract men who deny their masculine essence. If you have the, "I'm a strong black woman, I can do it on my own, and I don't need anybody" mindset, and project that through your essence, you will attract a f**k boy who does not want to protect or provide. A man with a masculine essence knows his primary role is to protect and provide. Not just financially but emotionally and spiritually as well. If a woman acts as if she does not need him, he will not find her attractive. Rachael Jayne Groover says, *"In fact, masculine men are much more drawn to women who love to receive their gifts, women who readily display that they have room in their life and a need for a partner.* The bottom line is, polarity must always be present in romantic relationships. Someone must possess the feminine essence, and someone must possess the masculine essence. It is always up to us which essence we will embrace and project. The woman who discards her feminine essence will find herself thoroughly disappointed. Although she projects a masculine essence, she is naturally feminine. When a f**k boy does not meet the needs of her feminine essence, she will end up frustrated and resentful for having to play the role of the man. She will resent having to carry the weight of the relationship and take on more of the masculine responsibility than she should. It is important to note the difference between a couple who share responsibilities to maintain a household and family. Dual earners are often necessary in today's society. When each individual maintains their natural essence to create a harmonious relationship there is no issue.

If you want to be f**k boy free and set yourself on the path to meet your masculine kindred spirit, you must fully embrace your feminine essence. David Deida, author of The Way of the Superior Man says, *"If a man is very masculine by nature, then he will be attracted to a very feminine woman, who will complement his energy...and if a man is more feminine by nature, his energy will be complemented by the strong direction and purposiveness of a more masculine woman"*. A f**k boy, either by nature of being more feminine or not being able to fully embrace his masculinity will not be attracted to feminine women. That is just the law of nature regarding polarity. When you fully embrace, learn to bask in and express your feminine essence you will only attract masculine men. Feminism (more on that in a later chapter) has tainted the power and joy of basking in the radiance of one's feminine essence. Feminine has become a dirty little word associated with weakness, powerlessness and being taken advantage of. We have rejected our feminine essence under the false sense that we are taking our power back. This belief has left us is lonely, bitter and going from one f**k boy to the next. We have become overworked, stressed, and disgruntled. We blame life, convinced that all the good men are taken, locked up in jail, or gay. But there are plenty of good men out there who are in search of their match and opposite, a woman who embraces and cultivates her feminine essence.

## Qualities of the Feminine Essence

The feminine essence is the most attractive and powerful force there is. It is also accessible by each woman. At the core of feminine essence is BEING. Jacqueline Whitmore, author of the book Poised for Success has emphasized that we are human beings, not human doings. A feminine woman will always be more focused on "being" rather than doing. Authenticity, vulnerability, magnetism, radiance, connection, unity and relationship are some terms that are associated with a feminine essence. The rhythm of the feminine essence is slower than the usual pace. Feminine essence is expressed through feelings rather than thoughts. A woman who is in tune with her feminine essence is guided by her intuition. She lives in harmony with her emotions and energy. She is an open conduit, easily open to receive as willingly as she gives. She is constantly in the flow of life. Her focus is inward, then outward. She is fully self-aware. She trusts herself completely and knows the power she possesses within. She is moved by the inner workings of her soul. She is mysterious and enigmatic. She is not easily understood or penetrated, but she lovingly allows others the opportunity to figure her out. She is an open book, but not easily read. The feminine essence is soft, fluid, flexible and circular (as opposed to linear). The feminine essence is in touch with Mother Nature and she looks to the moon, sun, plants, trees and animals for wisdom, guidance and relationship.

| Masculine Essence Qualities | Feminine Essence Qualities |
| --- | --- |
| Mind | Heart |
| Thinking | Feeling |
| Directive | Receptive |
| Reason | Imaginative |
| Logic & certainty | Intuition & the unknown |
| Go | Flow |
| Outcome | Process |
| External | Internal |
| Individual | Collective |

Have you turned off your feminine essence because society says that isn't how you get ahead? Have you been convinced that operating in the feminine will result in you being taken advantage of or played for the fool? Or maybe, you believe that it is impossible to operate in the feminine and get things done. Moving at a slower pace and being guided by our intuition isn't exactly deemed to be productive, at least not in this "dog-eat dog, get them before they get you, every man for himself", world we live in. Will operating in the feminine get you the pro-motion or corner office? Maybe it will or maybe it won't. This book isn't about getting ahead in a man's world. This book is about becoming a man's world. When it comes to masculine men, embracing your feminine essence is how you get the job done. David Deida explains, *"The feminine is the force of life. The more masculine a man is, the more his woman's feminine energy (as opposed to other qualities) will be important to him".* We have no choice but to reclaim and regenerate our feminine essence so that we can finally get the love, freedom, protection and provision that we deserve. It is time to be f**k boy free! It is time to begin to take tangible, practical steps to unearth and reconnect with your feminine essence. There are certain physical, energetic and emotional shifts in our lifestyle that will result in the embrace of our divine feminine essence. Rachael Jayne Groover wrote a great book on how to recon-nect with the feminine essence called, Powerful and Feminine. I would encourage to learn more about connecting to your feminine essence. Even a google search will result in many great articles about tapping into your feminine essence.

*Exercise: Movement is one way to embrace the femi-nine essence. Activities such as yin yoga, hula hooping, pole dancing and other non-competitive active sports will allow you to feel life through your body. You will flow easily and fluidly.*

*Slow down! Walk slower, move slower, let every act be an act of deliberate love. Stop rushing through life and through your day. Take moments to breathe. Take a moment to "be" instead of do. Release the tension in your shoulders and jaw. Remove your tongue from the roof of your mouth. Feel your body as it connects to the earth. When you walk, become aware of your move-ments. Take time throughout your day to go inward to connect with your intuition and energy. Be present in your physical body. Bring your breath and focus to your womb space daily.*

\* \* \*

*"Soften your heart and allow your love to shine"*

*Rachael Jayne Groover*

\* \* \*

# CHAPTER 3

# Express Feminine Energy

*"There is nothing more rare, nothing more beautiful, than a woman being unapologetically herself; comfortable in her perfect imperfection. To me, that is the true essence of beauty*

*Dr. Steve Maraboli*

In the prior chapter we learned that essence is who we are, and energy is how we express who we are. Energy by definition is "the impetus behind all motion and all activity". Energy is an intangible, modifiable force believed to emanate from a person, place or thing. Energy is a vibe, a feeling, an impression".

Energy is the way in which we do anything. I read once, *"How you do anything is how you do everything"*. Energy is in the how. Energy is the heart driving the action. Any woman can walk from point A to point B, but how does she walk from point A to point B? This is energy. Any woman can have a conversation and engage with a man, but how does she engage and converse with a man? This is energy. How does she make him feel when he is in her presence? This is energy. There's not much we can do about our essence. We are feminine in nature. Energy is more malleable. We can choose an energy to project. We can turn an energy on and off. It is important to express feminine energy because this vibe, feeling or impression is the easiest way to stay connected to your feminine essence. If you are currently disconnected from your feminine essence, expressing feminine energy will revive that connection. To be f**k boy free, we must express feminine energy in our interactions with men. The feminine energy we project is the easiest way for a man with a masculine essence to find us or in the case of f**k boys, to stay away from us. Most women are afraid to express feminine energy because they think that it makes them look weak. They fear being hurt or taken advantage of. This fear causes them to slow down or shut off the flow of feminine energy in their lives. Instead, they express masculine energy which they feel will protect them from being hurt, but to no avail. They become hardened and out of touch. Their radiance begins to shrivel like an old piece of fruit; ripe for f**k boy picking.

Pretending to be something you aren't won't protect you from getting hurt. Pretending as if you aren't a brutally soft woman won't guarantee you won't be rejected. Many of us have been in survival mode for a very long time. We don't know how to define ourselves beyond the pain, trauma and hurt. Our negative past experiences have become the lens from which we view life. We don't see life through rose-colored glasses, we see them through pain-colored glasses. As Rumi said, *"Your task is not to seek for love, but merely to seek and find all the barriers within yourself that you have built against it."* Expressing feminine energy helps to remove these barriers. I have always been a very sensitive, deep feeling person. But in order to protect myself, I use to pretend to be tougher than I was. I would be aggressive and cold in my interactions with men, using this energy as a defense mechanism. Because this energy did not match my feminine essence, an internal conflict ensued that caused me to be self-conscious and confused. This mix of energies was attractive to f**k boys. They thrive off women who are confused and lack self-confidence. This domino effect began with not being aligned with my feminine essence. The more connected you are with your feminine essence, the more feminine energy you exude.

How do you express feminine energy? Do what feels natural. Walk, move and speak as your intuition guides you. Soften and relax your facial muscles. Smile and release the tension in your shoulders. Pay attention to your breathing. Is it hurried or does the breath flow through your body easily? Bring your focus to your stomach/pelvic area which holds your womb. These are all things that will precipitate the free flow of feminine energy in your body. Go back to Chapter 2 and review the qualities of the feminine essence.

Everything we do comes from two sources and two sources only; love or fear. We are either living a fear-based reality or a love-based reality (more on that in a later chapter). Feminine energy is based on love. Love of self, first and foremost. When you live a love-based reality, you do not worry about what will happen in the future. For example, you may feel you want to do something for someone. You may want to give them a gift, a hug, a compliment or simply tell them how much they mean to you. Your initial reaction is to readily give that gift, but then fear-based thinking comes into play. What if they don't like it? Will others think I am doing too much? What if they don't reciprocate or show gratitude? What if they think this is an opening to take advantage of me? These thoughts cause you to second guess your initial desire to give. Then, you either give reluctantly or not at all, creating uncertainty within. This is not feminine energy. Feminine energy will say, "I was led to do this, and my heart is never wrong. I am not responsible for how people perceive me or receive what I give. I did what felt right to me in the moment and I feel good about it. I am at peace and this honors who I am". There is no attachment to the outcome. Expressing feminine energy is doing what honors you. Your actions, vibes and sentiments compliment and glorify who you are and makes you feel good. If giving makes you feel good, then give. If it honors who you are then do it. If expressing your deepest feelings and emotions through poetry, art, or dance honors who you are then do it. Operating in your feminine essence and expressing feminine energy is next level. Inevitably, when you reach this next level, you will meet others who are also next level. F**k boys do not operate at this level. However, masculine men will be on this level and they are deeply attracted to women who are comfortable expressing feminine energy. In February of 2019, I interviewed four men for a blog series on Alpha Males, hoping to gain some true insight into what a masculine man desires from women. I considered these men to be the cream of the crop when it comes to manhood. These were men that I personally knew and had great respect for. They were loyal, loving, family men who were protectors and providers. I asked them four questions to provide insight into what a man truly desires in a woman. One of the qualities that came up more than any other was confidence. A woman who knows who she is at the soul level and confidently expresses that was a quality the men said was a non-negotiable. A self-assured woman was a winner. One point they also brought up, which I greatly appreciated was that a woman didn't have to be perfect. She could still be a work in progress, striving to be better, do better and express herself more at the soul level and they would still find her equally as attractive.

> **Exercise**: List 3 feminine qualities that embody the core of who you are. They could include, gentleness, compassion, nurturance, sensitivity, intuitive, vulnerable, and artistic. For each quality, list one way you can begin to express that quality as energy on a daily basis. Then, express that energy through action to magnify your core feminine qualities.

# CHAPTER 4

# Use Masculine Energy Wisely

*"A woman will never out-male a man who is in his power"*

*Rachael Jayne Groover*

In order to be f**k boy free it is imperative to use masculine energy wisely. As the old saying goes, "you need to know when to hold them and when to fold them". A woman must know when to use masculine energy and when to deactivate it. Masculine energy should only be used in certain situations and to achieve certain goals. Masculine energy has great value. Masculine energy is the impetus used to achieve goals, go into warrior mode to protect ourselves and our families, and to navigate the working male-dominated world. Masculine qualities include logic, independence and assertiveness. Masculine energy will prove to be an impediment when attracting a masculine man. Instead, it will be an attractive force for a true f**k boy. A wise woman is one that basks in the radiance of her feminine essence. She prefers to express feminine energy, but she also understands that masculine energy can be useful. We should never rely on masculine energy or have it be our default energy mode. When a woman relies too heavily on masculine energy, she will not only be a magnet for f**k boys, she will also experience physical, spiritual and energetic dis-ease that will manifest in various ways. Rachael Jayne Groover says, *"If a woman's body runs a lot of masculine energy for a long time her body will burn out because most feminine bodies were not meant to run on masculine energy long-term. She may start to feel anger and resentment towards the world."*

I often think of our enslaved female ancestors who were fierce protectors and warriors. They had to exert a lot of masculine energy to survive MAAFA, the Black Holocaust. It took great strength, courage, and quick, rational thinking to survive the middle passage, slavery, sharecropping, Jim Crow and life in the urban ghetto. It also shows what has happened to the natural feminine essence of the black woman. She was not given the freedom to truly connect with and express her feminine essence. Hence the stereotype of the "angry black woman". But the black woman isn't angry, she is wounded, scarred and in need of deep healing. She uses her tough exterior as a defense mechanism to prevent further hurt and deeper wounds. We must develop the wisdom to know when masculine energy is appropriate and necessary, or we will continue the generational cycle of wounded women.

I exert masculine energy daily at work. I am often assertive and led by logic and rational thinking as opposed to my feelings. My focus is outward as opposed to inward, and it serves me well. I exerted masculine energy to write this book. I had to focus, set goals and be driven. I did not always feel like writing, but it was that inner drive that pushed me to open my laptop. The masculine force of "doing" helped me get the job done. I love lifting weights. It is another way I exert masculine energy. I feel strong and powerful. It is how I release tension and stress. When we set goals for ourselves or set out to complete a project or realize a dream, we often express masculine energy to see our dreams, goals and projects come to fruition. Masculine energy is useful in the board room, the court room, the classroom, and at the conference table. Masculine energy is rarely, if ever needed at home. We do not need masculine energy when we are with our men, children or families. We must leave the remnants of masculine energy at work. Our men have all the masculine energy we need. Our fathers, brothers, boyfriends, sons and husbands should not have to compete with us to see who can exert more masculine energy. F**k boys, on the other hand will let you win and will take on more of the feminine energy. Remember, polarity must exist in relationships. If you take on the masculine role, you will attract a man who is willing to take on the feminine role. If you embrace your feminine essence, exert feminine energy and use masculine energy wisely, you will attract a man who has a primary masculine essence. If you meet a lot of men in your job or career, it is important that you turn off masculine energy immediately when you are not in a work setting or a work situation that requires masculine energy. The truly masculine man will greatly appreciate your ability to use masculine energy wisely while not sacrificing your natural feminine essence. The key to success in using masculine energy wisely will occur when you can create harmony between the masculine and feminine energy that circulates in your vibratory aura. There must be harmony between being (feminine) and doing (masculine).

I dated a guy once who I considered to be a weak man. I had very little respect for him. He seemed incapable of running his life without the slightest bit of guidance. His child's mother mistreated him, and I used to tell him how he had to stand up to her. He started to rely on me for daily advice on how to navigate his co-parenting relationship. He was a true f**k boy. How did I end up dating him? Without going into the specifics of how we met, we were opposites. At that time in my life, I was not connected to my feminine essence and I exerted a lot of masculine energy. He was a man who was disconnected from his masculine essence and exerted a lot of feminine energy. Polarity existed and we connected. I became very frustrated in our interactions. The reason I was frustrated was because although I was exerting a lot of masculine energy by leading him in what to do and say, that was not in line with my natural feminine essence. My needs were not being met. I did not want to be in a relationship with a man who did not know how to direct his own life. I started to assume that role for him and

I resented him for it. As a woman with a feminine essence, I wanted to be the nurturer and nourisher, not the leader. I did not want to determine the path but be able to provide the spiritual and emotional provision needed on the path. I was more than willing to give advice, guidance and my occasional "two cents", but not the way I was doing it. It was as if I was his mentor or life coach. I did not use my masculine energy wisely and I paid dearly for it. His child's mother eventually got wind of all my "advice" and lashed out at me and I ended up having to defend myself in court.

The stereotype of the "strong" black woman has a very negative connotation. The "strong" black woman misuses masculine energy. If the "strong" black woman was using masculine energy correctly, then she would not be stressed, overwhelmed, fatigued, and embittered. When you operate at this level of masculine energy, you appear to be in competition with men and this is a huge turn off. True power and strength lie in a woman being who she innately is and expressing it fearlessly. There is no power in pretending to be something you are not. Most of us are brutally soft, yet we feel we cannot express this freely. Instead, we pretend to be tougher than we are. I feel most powerful and strong when I can be vulnerable and authentic. I feel peace when I can admit that I am tired, overwhelmed and in dire need of a break. I feel in control when my emotions can flow freely and I do not have to keep them bottled up, shoved down or swept under the rug. Have you ever wondered how masculine men can easily let things go? Nothing seems to bother them. Masculine energy compartmentalizes That is one of the ways masculine energy circulates within them. We are not wired that way. We must be free to flow and feel. And there is nothing wrong with that. Imagine if an ant was told to fly from flower to flower and pollinate. The ant would fail miserably and feel inadequate. But only because the ant was attempting to do something it wasn't designed to do. That is what happens when women misuse their masculine energy and rely too heavily on it. They will feel like they are failing at life and in their relationships with men.

While I am driven to accomplish goals and conquer feats, this is only some of the time. Most times I'd rather not be in warrior mode. It's exhausting and depletes me of my energy. It's exhausting to build walls around my heart. It is exhausting to carry a chip on my shoulder. It is exhausting to be in a constant mode of "go", like a hamster on a hamster wheel. I do not want to take over the world. I want to master the world within and let my light shine. At times it may require masculine energy, but often I must connect with my divine feminine essence and go inward. Mastering when and when not to use masculine energy will be key in being f**k boy free. Success begins and ends with you.

> *Exercise*: Identify and write down one area in your life where masculine energy is useful for your overall success. Commit to using masculine energy in that one area only. Begin to take steps to use feminine energy in every other area of your life.

# CHAPTER 5

# Become the Woman of Your Dreams

*"Sometimes, the man of your dreams is on the next level of where you need to be as a woman"*

*Unknown*

As women, we are quick to pull out our lists of requirements, standards, expectations, non-negotiables and deal breakers when it comes to the men we desire. They must have a certain look, have a certain amount of money and possess a myriad of other qualities if they want to be in our lives. And while I fully support knowing what you are looking for in a man and what your deal breakers are, some women can take it too far. They want a man who is over 6 foot, in good shape, makes six figures, and is understanding, kind and can give some good D. But I have a very important question. Would the man of your dreams consider you to be the woman of his dreams? I'll take it a step further. We want a man who is kind to us, but are we kind to ourselves? We desire a man with ambitions and goals, but do we have goals? We desire a man who accepts and loves us unconditionally, but do we love and accept ourselves unconditionally? We desire a man with a certain level of physical and sexual attraction, but do we work to maintain a level of physical and sexual attraction? If you want to be f**k boy free and attract your kindred masculine spirit, then you must become the woman of your dreams. It sounds cliché but falling deeply and madly in love with yourself is a sure-fire way to be f**k boy free. F**k boys love women who don't know who they are and have low self-esteem. They love women who don't think they deserve good men and will settle for anyone who gives them a compliment or shows them attention. This used to be me. I struggled with assessing my self-worth. F**k boys could see this from miles away and they came running to my rescue. A f**k boy knows when a woman has low standards and knows that there is a lot he can get away with. A woman who does not love herself will not hold a man accountable. She will accept anything he gives her, even if it is abuse, infidelity and betrayal.

You must become the woman of your dreams. You must become a woman you are immensely proud of. You should enjoy spending time with yourself and find comfort and joy in your own presence. Warsan Shire says, *"My alone feels so good, I'll only have you if you're sweeter than my solitude"*. It is a beautiful feeling to be in this space. This will allow only the best of men with the purest of intentions to share space with you and to partake of your energy and be worthy of your time. Writer Ava explains, *"hold company with yourself so sacred that even when you are alone, you are whole"*. This is so vitally important to be f\*\*k boy free. I used to avoid being alone as much as possible. I could not stand to be alone with my thoughts because they haunted me. I had to have a man with me at night. I had to converse with a man daily. That need allowed f\*\*k boys access to me and eventually into my life. Until I learned to love myself and my time alone, I attracted f\*\*k boys who could not love me, because I did not love myself. It has been said that we teach others how to treat us by how we treat ourselves. If we abuse ourselves, neglect ourselves, and speak negatively to ourselves, we are showing others exactly how to treat us.

Becoming the woman of your dreams means loving and accepting yourself completely. It means making decisions that honor the core of who you are and engaging in activities that make you feel proud. When you become the woman of your dreams, your primary objective is to embody self-love and practice radical self-care. Above all, you must become your own best friend. You must always pour into your cup first. Of course, this is easier said than done, but it must become your daily goal. You will never meet the man of your dreams if you don't meet the woman of your dreams in the mirror first. If you are like me, this can be a long and arduous journey. But it does get easier with time. The more you commit to yourself, it will become less of a chore and something you love to do. As a child I was told that I was ugly, that no one liked me and that I was mean. I believed these lies and embraced them as truth. It was easy for any man who said I was beautiful easy access to me. Because I did not believe I was beautiful or worthy any man who showed interest I most likely gave a chance. This allowed f**k boys to enter my life. I have fought like hell to release the lies I was told and embrace the inherent truth of who I was; beautiful, enough and worthy. This meant digging deep, revisiting the past multiple times, using affirmations, releasing weight and developing a beauty routine that made me love the woman staring back at me in the mirror.

\* \* \*

*"I love myself'. The quietest. Simplest.*
*Most powerful revolution ever"*

*Unknown*

\* \* \*

If you struggle with low self-esteem and find it hard to see the value and worth of your being, you may grapple with questions like, how do I love myself? Or what can I do to love and accept myself more? A favorite quote of mine is by @fictionista. She says, *"I've loved many. Yet if I could go back and start over, the first person I would have learned to love would be myself"*. Self-love is the key. One of the first steps to becoming the woman of your dreams is to identify your most beautiful and endearing qualities. One of the best books I've read is, *The*

*15 Invaluable Laws of Growth* by John C. Maxwell. In this book he states, "Self-esteem is the single most significant key to a person's behavior". In his book there was an exercise where you had to write down 100 things you liked about yourself. Honestly, I struggled after number 10. But eventually I wrote down 100 things I liked about myself; from my strong work ethic, to the shape of my eyes to the intensity and passion of my soul. I still have that list and I look at it from time to time to remind myself, yes, I am indeed the shit. Becoming committed to personal growth is very important to become the woman of your dreams. Commit every day to being better than you were yesterday. Be brave enough to face your fears. This will breed self-confidence and self-trust. I love taking personality assessments. They help me to learn more about who I am and what my personal strengths are. I would urge you to get to know yourself. Assessments like the Myers Briggs Personality Assessment (I am an INFJ by the way), Strength Finders and How the World Sees You are great places to start. I guarantee, the more you learn about what makes you, uniquely you, you will love yourself a lot more.

It is equally important to also identify the things that you would like to change. This may seem counterproductive, but it will serve a purpose. There was a time I didn't like the way I looked physically; I was not happy with my weight, my skin or my over-all image. I also didn't like my quick- tempered attitude and the way I would let certain things and people trigger me. I didn't like that I was driven by fear. A fear of what others thought of me (admittedly, I am a recovering people pleaser), a fear of failure and even a fear of success. To become the woman of my dreams, there were some things that had to change. There were some mindsets I had to discard, some habits I needed to break and some new habits I needed to implement in my life. There will be some things you must change as well. It is never easy to admit that there are some areas where you need to grow. It can be an uncomfortable feeling, but it must be done. Sit with those feelings and emotions that come to the surface when you think about the areas you need to improve. This is not to berate ourselves, tear ourselves down or have a pity party. This is to get a clear picture of the areas of our lives that need improvement.

Over the past 5 years I have spent thousands of dollars on books, classes, certifications, workout equipment, organic food, and whatever else I needed to enhance my strengths and improve my weak areas. At one point I got tired of looking in the mirror and not being fully pleased with what was looking back at me. I decided to transform my body into a master-piece. I joined weight watchers in 2010. After I had my daughter in 2011 and gained all the weight back and then some, I got myself back on track. I stopped eating fast food and drinking pop/soda. I asked my dad if he would teach me how to lift weights, and I put my jogging stroller to good use. I bought books and took online classes on how to enhance my internal and external beauty. I stopped making excuses as to why I couldn't be the woman of my dreams and decided to BECOME the woman of my dreams. The more I focused on personal growth and development, I began to love myself. I loved what I was learning about health and wellness and I decided to pursue a certification so I could help others. I invested in myself again. It was a domino effect. I just had to make that first move. And here I am, loving myself more than I ever imagined, and every day I am learning to love myself more. But changing the outside was so much easier than changing the inside. Dealing with my resentment, anger, bitterness and self-sabotaging ways was a process indeed. I found books on self-healing and began my journey of discovering the ancestral wisdom that lay dormant to deal with my demons, shadows and fears. For some, counseling may be the investment you need to mend what's broken.

Go back to school or fire your boss and start that business. Write that book, create that work of art. Grow a garden or take that dream vacation you've always wanted. Find a new hobby, release the excess weight you've been carrying, and start paying off your debt. Quit smoking, leave your husband or long-time boyfriend. End that toxic friendship or relationship. Do something you've always wanted to do but were too afraid to do. Do whatever it is that will make you feel proud and free. Fall in love with yourself and your life. Create a life that you love.

It is also important to rewire the brain with positive affirmations. If you aren't in control of your thoughts, negative self-talk will destroy you. Gautama Buddha said, *"All that we are is the result of what we have thought. We are made of our thoughts; we are molded by our thoughts"*. You must be proactive in counteracting all the negativity that exists in your conscious and sub-conscious mind. It may not even be your own voice that you hear. Maybe its family or bullies who said mean and negative things about you. Maybe you were told your nose or lips were too big, or you were too dark, too light, or your hair was too nappy or short. Maybe you were told you weren't going to amount too much, or you were like what people considered to be your no-good mother or father. Maybe your childhood crush rejected you and you have felt unworthy and unlovable since then. It could be several things. It could be anything. But you must not allow those thoughts to roam free in your mind. You must squelch these thoughts with positive affirmations. Positive affirmations have helped me to create new thought patterns and mindsets that serve the woman I want to become. I write them on post-it notes and put them on my mirror or the wall. I repeat them over and over, and when a negative thought comes in my mind, I destroy it with a positive affirmation. It has been said that *"positive affirmations are like vitamins for your mind"*.

When you become the woman of your dreams, you will become f**k boy free. You won't settle for a f**k boy's half-ass love because you are overflowing with self-love and acceptance. Their compliments, while graciously accepted won't be needed to feed your ego and build your self-esteem. You won't need his affirmations or validation because you have your own. The man of your dreams, your kindred spirit, will be drawn to the self-love that emanates from your being. He will readily participate in loving you the way you love yourself. A f**k boy will have no clue and by default he won't stand a chance in your presence.

* * *

*"I am new here. To this self-love. To this whole love. To this not changing for anyone, not apologizing to anyone, sort of kind and pure love. And I am never leaving"*

*Alison Malee*

* * *

**Exercise***: Write down 100 things you love about yourself. The exercise is not complete until you reach 100. If you must stop and come back that is ok. But write down 100 things. Next, identify three things you will do daily to improve you physical, mental, spiritual or financial health. This can be exercising, meditating, journaling, drinking half your body weight in ounces of water. You can read a self-help book before bed or start saving money by bringing lunch from home. These are all examples of things that can be done daily to improve ourselves. If you would like to focus on losing weight, fat and inches visit www.TFL28.com*

# CHAPTER 6

# Heal Your Womb

*"When a flower doesn't bloom you fix the environment in which it grows, not the flower"*

*Alexander Der Heijer*

If your womb has been wounded and unhealed, then you will be a magnet to f**k boys. At the age of 4, I was molested. The abuse went on for 7 years and ended when I was 11. Although the acts ended, the pain never stopped. I never said a word to anyone until I was in my twenties. At the age of 4, my fragile, innocent womb took its first crushing blow. When I was 18, it took its next and almost final fatal blow.

The woman's womb is the seat of her creativity. It holds the key to her magic, power, unique beauty and divinity. Dr. Philip Valentine, author of The Wounded Womb explains, "The womb is the dark-matter core of her universe. Her body is ruled by it-ruled by the mind of her 'womb-niverse'. It is the center and circumference of all her 'issues'". When a woman's womb has been wounded, she will struggle to find her place in the world and define herself. This inability to self-identify will place her in a very vulnerable state where others will find it easy to project their fears and insecurities onto her. Her womb will become the dumping ground for f**K boys to offload their pain and frustration. We must learn to not let *"f**k boys find calm and refuge in between your thighs".* Having a wounded womb means you have become accustomed to the exchange of trauma. Being treated less than you deserve becomes normal. Being abandoned, rejected, used, violated and disrespected becomes the norm in your relationships. And to survive, you find comfort in the familiarity of pain.

The womb of women who have experienced childhood molestation or rape has been violated. But you do not have to be the victim of sexual abuse to have your womb wounded. The rejection or denial of your femininity or your right to exist could also result in a wounded womb. You may have been told that you are too loud, too wild or too free. You may have grown up in a very strict home where your freedom was restricted. Anything that has denied your right to exist exactly as you are is a violation to your womb. I grew up in church where I was constantly subjected to the rules of "holiness" and righteous living. I could only wear skirts to church. They couldn't be too short or too tight. I was constantly told to keep my legs closed and not have sex until I was married. Sex was considered nasty and sinful. I was made to feel that my inherent sensuality and sexuality was a bad thing that had to be hidden, repressed and denied. I was left confused about what it meant to be a woman. This was another violation to the womb.

Our parents and caregivers subconsciously project their life experiences onto us. As our primary socializing agents, their fears become our fears. Their belief systems become our belief systems. And their experiences become our experiences. Maybe our mothers, grandmothers and aunts experienced trauma to their wombs and we carry the violation of their wombs trans generationally. For example, maybe your mother was raped, and she holds the belief that men cannot be trusted. She projects that belief onto you, and you carry that with you even though you may not have had that experience. But because you hold that belief, eventually you will experience a situation that makes the belief, "men can't be trusted" a truth. There are various ways our wombs can be wounded. Disappointment, shame, fear, guilt are all emotions that will wound our wombs. Cultural and religious conditioning, and societal expectations can wound the womb. Because our wombs are where our intuitive power reside, a wounded womb will disconnect you from the inherent knowledge every woman has access to. Instead, you will be forced to rely on a world that is all too eager to tell a black woman who she is.

A wounded womb can manifest in many ways. Long heavy periods, cramps, fibroids and infertility are just some of the symptoms our body manifests to alert us that healing is needed. We deepen the wound when we let f**k boys inside of us. By nature, we are receivers. We open to receive all that men have to offer; the good and the bad. A f**k boy will offer up pain. A masculine man will offer healing and peace. If your womb is accustomed to pain, a f**k boy will feel normal. But a healed womb, balanced and free will not allow a f**k inside. The woman with a healed womb knows that a f**k boy will taint the temple that has been nourished and healed with positive affirmations and radical self-care. To truly be f**k boy free, you must heal your womb. You must go back to the source of your pain and anguish and deal with it. Yes, it will be painful. Yes, it will take time. Yes, you will shed many gut wrenching tears. But it will be worth it when the f**k boy who used to dick you down so good you no longer have a desire for. I saw a post on Instagram that said, *"If my spirit rejects you, my pussy will too"*. You no longer desire him, because you realize you were simply using him to continue the cycle of trauma you had become accustomed to. You have broken the cycle and he is no longer needed. There was a time where I did not honor myself, nor I did not honor my womb. My childhood trauma had nearly destroyed me. But when I got sick and tired of being used by f**k boys and the "hit it and quit it" experiences, I decided that something needed to change. But I didn't quite know where to start. One of my favorite quotes is from the book The Alchemist. The author says, *"And when you want something, all the universe conspires in helping you to achieve* *it"*. I wanted better. I wanted more and so the universe set me on a path that has led to me being able to heal my womb.

In 2007, I was unemployed and without a car after graduating top of my class with a BS in Accounting and BA in Sociology. I was also overweight and still dealing with the loss of my first love and my first child. To say I was depressed was an understatement. I used to walk to the library and get four or five books at a time. I came across one book that talked about black women and low self- esteem. Sadly, I cannot remember the name of that book, but it said that we must identify who taught us to hate ourselves. A lightbulb went off. At four years old, my abuser taught me to hate myself. I thought my interactions with him were normal; filled with pain, pleasure and then more pain. I searched for my abuser in every man I met. My abuser reincarnated in every f**k boy I had a relationship with. This was my normal. Being used for sex. Being abandoned, rejected and ultimately unloved. After reading that book, I started my healing journey. 12 years later and I'm still healing the varied layers of my past.

I would like to emphasize that you don't have to wait until you are completely and fully healed to find the man of your dreams. Are we ever fully and completely healed? I have often blogged about the layers of healing that must be undertaken. You never "arrive". There is always more healing to do, more karma to transcend and deeper ways to practice self-love. Like me, you may find your kindred spirit while you are in the midst of healing. He may come along and love you while you are learning to love yourself. My partner often jokes about how much he loves my troubled soul. When I have my moments of fear, doubt, and depression when revisiting my past, he will say, "it's ok babe. I know you are having a troubled soul moment". He will often comment on my growth and tell me how proud of me he is. There is a man who will give you the understanding and patience that you need on your healing journey. Life rewards us for our hard work. The universe is madly in love with a woman who is brave enough to put the pieces of her life back together. That reward can manifest as a man who loves both the healed and broken parts of you.

When we are unhealed and refuse to address the underlying core issues that result in our dysfunction, we will attract men who will gladly participate in the drama that is our lives. A f**k boy will become the modern-day version of your abuser, rapist, parent, religious institution, caregiver, relative, teacher or whoever else wounded your womb. We must become 100% responsible for the current state of our lives. No, we are not at fault for the pain others have inflicted onto us. No, it is not my fault that I was violated as a child. But I am responsible today for what happens in my life and my future. I take my power back and choose to heal. As Sarah Jakes Roberts said, *"You're responsible for how long you let what hurt you, haunt you.*

Self-care is one of the best ways to begin to heal the womb. I don't mean shopping sprees, massages and getting your hair and nails done. As Jacqueline Whitmore said, "Self-care is not self-indulgence". I am talking about spending some real time with yourself. Taking the time to reflect and sit in quiet and solitude to rest and relax. Fasting (from food, people and social media), meditating, vaginal steaming, spiritual baths, yin- yoga, therapy, and journaling are ways that I have been able to practice self-care. I had to go back and rescue my 4-year-old self. I had to hold her and tell her how worthy she is, how beautiful she is and that I will always protect her. I had to save myself, for myself, by myself. I had to go back to my 18-year-old self and tell her how proud I am of her graduating college, finding a job and for never giving up when she had every reason to quit. At 35 years old I go back to rescue the younger versions of myself and mold us together to live out the glorious future we have all dreamed of. You must fight for your healing, and you must fight for yourself. Not with bitterness and anger towards others, but with a sense of radical and rebellious self-love that believes you are worthy even though the world tells you otherwise. One of my absolute favorite quotes is by Upile Chisala. She says, *"I have loved myself out of so much bullshit".*

*Exercise: Find a quiet space and sit. Take three deep breaths with your eyes closed. Afterward, I want you to ask yourself out loud, "Who taught me to hate myself? Who taught me that I was unworthy, unloved and did not have value? Write the incidents, experiences and people that come to your mind. Afterwards (it may be a few minutes or a few hours), decide if you are ready to take the next steps in the healing process. You may not be ready at this time. Let your intuition guide you on how to proceed. But remember, just because you bury it, doesn't mean it's dead.*

\* \* \*

*"Self-love will save your soul"*

\* \* \*

# CHAPTER 7

# Don't Be A Feminist

*"Each woman knew that she held the destiny of many people in her hands. This is what made women great"*

*Puma LaGuitana*

\* \* \*

*"Feminine women have more power than a woman trying to be a man"*

*Unknown*

This book is not male bashing. It is not to denigrate men and highlight the ways in which they have failed us. This book is a tool to empower women to attract that which they deeply deserve and desire. No, we don't want f**k boys! But yes, we LOVE our men. We desire to connect and share space with wonderful masculine men who will protect and provide. Men who understand our feminine essence and give us the freedom to create and move in ways that honor who we are. We yearn to connect with our kindred spirit who will support us, inspire us and listen to us. We long to connect deeply on all levels, including spiritually and sexually. I have often said I desire to be both drowned and saved by a man. I want to be immersed in a man's love and power as I flow deeply in my own love and power. I respect the man as the head of our family, but I also understand that while he leads, I lay the path with the power and strength of my feminine essence. A truly feminine woman who is connected to her intuition and healed womb knows that she is the force that drives all.

This type of thinking is not in line with feminist thought. I find feminist thought to be an impediment to women fulfilling their desires. Feminist thinking will cause a f**k boy to fall right in your lap. Feminist thinking is very dangerous when it comes to establishing relationships with masculine men. I believe that feminism is partly to blame for the preponderance of single black women and single black mothers in our communities.

A 2019 article published in Vox; a research- based policy analysis and commentary from economists discussed the black-white differences in marriage in the US. The statistics reveal that, "67% of white women between the ages of 25 and 54 were married, while only 34% of black women were -a gap of 33 percentage points". This gap has steadily increased since 1980. The article continues stating, "In 2015, about 54% of black children lived with a single mother, while the share of white children living with a single mother was about 22%". Why are the majority of black women single and/or raising their children alone?

The intricacy of this discussion is beyond the parameters of this book. There are various independent factors that contribute to these alarming statistics. These factors include the high incarceration rates of black men, systematic racism and the transgenerational trauma of slavery. These are factors that are relatively out of our sphere of influence. But our ideologies and belief systems are within our sphere of influence and we have complete control over them. I would like to delve into the ideology of feminism and its association with f**k boys. This chapter ties into chapters 2, 3 and 4 which discuss feminine and masculine energy and feminine essence. Feminist thought is in direct contrast to these ideals. To be honest, I think that feminism is an ideology that black women need to sever ties with completely. It is a concept that was created by our white counterparts to address the issues they had with *their* men. They wanted more power, freedom, and independence; in their homes, the political arena and economically. They felt oppressed and stifled by patriarchy. They wanted the right to vote, the right to buy and sell property and they wanted the right to direct their own lives. They want equal pay and the opportunity to do whatever a man does. I am in no position to judge their rationale or feelings. Because I am not a white woman.

As a black woman I know that historically the black man is not the cause of the oppression and subjugation that I have experienced in this country. It is not the black man who physically enslaved me, raped me, sold my children, lynched my father, brother, husband, son or uncle. It is not the black man who has systematically denied my access to the available resources in society. It has been white society, and that includes both white men and women. White women have benefited from the enslavement of black men, women and children. A pivotal book titled, They Were Her Property by Stephanie E. Jones-Rogers, discusses white women slave owners in the American south. As a collective, white women are not the damsels in distress they portray themselves to be. When it comes to the politics of feminism and feminist thought, as a black woman I must ask myself why I would adhere to an ideology that doesn't support me as a black woman? Black women have worked the fields without pay for hundreds of years, making both white men and women rich. As a collective, white women stood idly by while their husbands, fathers and sons raped us and left us to raise their children in the slave quarters. It wasn't just white men who beat us, whipped us, and gave orders to lynch or for families to be separated by selling one or more family members. It was white women too. We were sold to pay for their wedding dresses or the furniture and other tangible goods they just had to have. Where is the sisterhood in that? Fast forward a few hundred years and they want to enter the workforce, the board room, the political arena and break glass ceilings. And they want the black woman to join forces with them. They want black women to abandon their men, children and communities and fight with them for their cause. Dr. Philip Valentine explains, *"what the neo-feminist really wants is to share in the white male's power structure my sister-not to change the power equation!"*

The black women's loyalty belongs to herself first (self-care), the black man and the black community. The black woman's ally and partner in the fight for black empowerment is the black man. The black man is not the enemy. He is the love of our life, our partner and friend. This is not to ignore the issues we have in our communities and home. This is to say that our ideologies should be black first. When discussing white feminists, Dr. Valentine explains, *"Her actual mission all along was to help destroy the black male's image in the eyes of the black female, thus undermining and destroying the archetypal bonds of trust and dependency that held the black team together as a family".*

How does this factor into the discussion of being f**k boy free? Our ideologies impact our choices of men. If we adopt feminist thought, then we view men and ourselves in a certain light. Feminist thought paints women as scorned victims with battles to fight against men. Feminist thought is especially dangerous for black women because it mistakenly paints black men as the oppressor and the impediment when in reality that is just not true. There are some women who say things like, "all men are dogs", "all men want is for women to be barefoot and pregnant" or "men only want one thing". These statements are rooted in feminist thought. Your reality will mirror your belief system. The universe will gladly give you that which you believe. This is how the law of attraction works. If you accept statements like those mentioned above, the attraction for f**k boys is intensified. You must view men as the Kings and Gods that they are. Your belief system must be one that causes you to make statements like, "there are good men out there who are loving and loyal". Because there are! There are men out there who will love the shit outta you. But does your ideology support that statement? I always say, "the black man is god", because that is how I view black men. But not all men are gods and we will discuss that in the next chapter. This is to illustrate that my belief system supports that there are good men out there. I do not believe that patriarchy is stopping me from doing and being anything I want to do and be. When I look up, I do not see a glass ceiling, I see endless possibilities and opportunities available to me. I do not believe that patriarchy is pulling me back into the stone age where women are barefoot and pregnant. I wouldn't mind being barefoot and pregnant, in my garden at home picking fresh herbs and vegetables for dinner. I want to know what it feels like to serve my family instead of slaving on the corporation plantation.

Feminist thinking is unattractive to men with a masculine essence. They will not stay to fight you when they already must fight the racist systems of American society. Your degrees and six figure salary will not keep him. A masculine man is not impressed by your ability to climb the corporate ladder. He will be more impressed by your ability to complement his masculine essence. A f**k boy will stick around for a while; get what he can, take what he wants and then leave. Feminism will not serve a woman who wants to avoid f**k boys and attract a masculine man. If you want to be f**k boy free, then you need to give feminism back to the white woman who gave it to you.

*Exercise*: Write down the first three things that come to your mind when the following question is asked, "what is your perception of black men"? Look at those three perceptions and identify if your statements are rooted in feminist thought. If they are, ask yourself if those belief systems are in alignment with your desire to be f**k boy free and in a loving relationship with a masculine man. The exercises in chapters 2, 3, and 4 will help to address any issues that come up in this exercise.

# CHAPTER 8

# Don't Ignore Red Flags: You Cannot Change Him

*"Consider how hard it is to change yourself and you'll understand what little chance you have in trying to change others"*

*Unknown*

* * *

*"Don't try to change people. Just love them. Love is what changes us"*

*Unknown*

Yes, the black man is god. But not all men know this to be true about themselves and conduct themselves in a godly manner. If you want to be f\*\*k boy free, then you cannot make the mistake of seeing something in a man that he doesn't see in himself. You cannot choose a man based on what he could be. You must choose him as he is. You cannot change him. A man must forge his own path. Just as you must become the woman of your dreams, he must become the man of his dreams. You will continually break your heart if you entertain f\*\*k boys with potential. I saw a post on Instagram that spoke volumes to this topic. The post says:

*"Women often enter into relationships trying to cook their way, sex their way, force their way, serve their way, submit their way into a man's heart to prove their worth. All to be chosen...we fight to open him up, soften him up, earn his trust, be the mother he never had, show him the loyalty he has never received, overlook the red flags because he has potential, be his therapist, settle for a mediocre courtship, settle for lackluster sex, settle for selfishness and no reciprocity..."*

I'm sure that we have all seen posts on social media from women who bash their baby fathers or exes, lamenting about how they aren't any good while highlighting his failures and shortcomings. I've been guilty of doing the same (but not on social media). The truth is, I knew very early on in the relationship with my child's father that he had the potential to not be shit. If we are being completely honest with ourselves, every woman who has complained about a f\*\*k boy knew he was a f\*\*k boy and was possibly going to fail her. The signs and the red flags are always there; loud and clear, but often we choose to ignore them or minimize them. Something feels off and our intuition alerts us, but we choose to see this man as something he's not and then get upset when he does what we knew he was capable of doing in the first place.

If a man shows signs of being abusive, being unfaithful, of emotional and financial instability, those signs should not be ignored. Eventually, they will manifest into full blown behavior patterns. A woman cannot change a man. If he is struggling financially, no matter how many job prospects you send him, if he doesn't desire better, then he won't do better. If he demonstrates that he is emotionally immature no matter how much you nurture him, if he doesn't have a desire to be vulnerable then he will continue to detach. I saw signs in my daughter's father that he had addictive tendencies, but I ignored these signs. It wasn't until months later when I was pregnant that it became clear that not only was he an alcoholic but used drugs as well. I would downplay his faults and focus on the good things. Yes, he drank every day, but at least he was home and not laid up with some other woman. I was in deep denial.

Being f**k boy free means being completely honest with yourself about the men you allow in your life. You must accept all that he is no matter how handsome or sexy he is. Don't allow yourself to get dick whipped and ignore the fact that he has absolutely nothing else to offer. I know this through experience. Years ago, I stopped to get some gas and went inside to pay. There was this man at the counter making his transaction, we made eye contact and it was love at first sight. He was fine! He was 6'3, black as night, had the most amazing body and chiseled facial features. His smile was so bright, teeth perfect and his voice was so sexy. He was charming, funny and sweet. He picked me up and we went on our first date. The entire night was perfect, and I just knew he was going to be my future husband. On the drive home he mentioned something about having to take the car back. I barely heard what he said. I was too busy planning the next 20 years of our lives together. Over the next couple of weeks, I found out he did not have a car, he was living with his mother and he was unemployed. He was really struggling. Before he found a job, I tried to help him any way I could. Meanwhile, I was living in LaLa land with the ideal of what he could be and the life we could have, instead of accepting the reality of who he was and the life we would never have. We had many arguments and disagreements because of my disappointments and unmet expectations. But the truth is, he tried to tell me on our first date, but I was too blind to accept reality. Yes, I wonder why he would pursue a woman or get involved in a relationship when he didn't have a job or car and was still trying to forge his own path. But I must also ask why I would continue to be involved with a man who had nothing to offer. We were both wrong. But because I can only control myself, I can only attempt to right my wrongs.

This is not to bash men who are struggling financially, mentally or emotionally. We all struggle. This is about recognizing where people are and accepting it. You must honor the path they have chosen. You must offer them love, understanding and grace to figure out their life, on their own, without you. You do not have to stick around to see if a f**k boy will change. You are not obligated to participate in struggle love with f**k boys. If he changes and he wants you he will find you. Release him in love, which can be hard to do. We are nurturers by nature. Many of us are quick to offer a helping hand, and so many of our black men need our love and support. But this must be done with wisdom and with a no strings attached approach. You cannot have ulterior motives. If you are going to help a man, then help him as sister helps a brother. Stop giving with the expectation that he is going to offer you loyalty, love, a ring or marriage one day. Stop looking at men like the build a bear workshop where you can pick and choose which qualities you want him to have. You can't take the good and leave the bad. Men are not here for our pleasure only. It is important to not view men as dispensable, interchangeable parts in our lives. They are people too. There came a point where I had to ask myself if I truly wanted a relationship. Or did I just want a big fancy ring and wedding. I had to ask myself if I truly wanted to build a bond and connection with a man, or did I just want someone to go to dinner with, post pictures on social media and have sex with. It was eye opening. Doing this allowed me to look at my past relationships with more compassion and grace. Being f**k boy free means recognizing f**k boys for who they are in all their f**k boy glory and releasing them to figure out life on their own without you.

You are not obligated to anyone but yourself. You are not obligated to help a man tap into his potential. You are not obligated to stick around with the hope that things will improve when your intuition is telling you otherwise. You must decide if he is worth it. F**k boys are never worth it.

*Exercise*: Start establishing clear boundaries for everyone in your life. Practice saying no to things that you don't want to do. Practice declining invitations to events, to join organizations, or to volunteer if you don't want to go or join. Get in the habit of saying no without offering an explanation. "No" is a complete sentence.

# CHAPTER 9

# Let Your Heart Be Home

*"Men need mental and emotional support too.
Not just pussy"*

*Unknown*

\* \* \*

*"For others he was just another HIM.
But for her, he was her only HYMN"*

*Wewake*

Being f**k Boy free means understanding your purpose in a man's life. I mentioned in the last chapter that I had to ask myself why I wanted to be in a relationship. I realized that I wanted to be in a relationship for all the wrong reasons. Most of my reasons were selfish. I wanted a piece of arm candy. I was often told that it would be very hard for me to find someone because I was too "difficult". I wanted to prove everyone wrong. Having a man would fulfill my need for external validation. But I also wanted someone to be there for me; but only when I needed him. I wanted to be able to spend time with someone; but only when I wanted to spend time with him. I wanted someone to help me problem solve and be a listening ear, but that was only when I couldn't figure things out on my own. I had a desire to get married, but I wanted a beautiful ring and a platinum wedding (I used to love watching that show). I didn't want a relationship; I wanted a lackey. It's no surprise I recycled f**k Boys. I had no real clue of what a real relationship looked like. A masculine, alpha male would have quickly recognized that I was only in it for selfish, external reasons and would not even bother. A f**k Boy wouldn't care one way or the other, if he could get something for himself in the process, he was good.

During my three-year process of implementing these 10 steps in my life and before meeting my kindred spirit, I had the pleasure of dating a West African man who taught me one of the most important lessons of my life. He taught me that my heart was a home. He taught me what it meant to be selfless and fearless in giving of myself and my love to a man. And he taught me this through heartbreak and rejection. He pursued me for some time, but I wasn't interested. I was casually dating someone at the time but when things were ending with the current man I was dating, we started talking more. He told me bits and pieces about his life in West Africa and how he ended up in Buffalo, NY. It was a fascinating story and the more time we spent together, the more I enjoyed his company. He explained that his family was very traditional, and they did not understand why he chose to come to America. He also told me that they had chosen a woman for him to marry and eventually he would travel home and fulfill his obligation. I asked him what would happen if he said no. He said that wasn't an option unless he wanted to bring shame on the family and possibly be disowned. He would have to marry her. What did I do? Of course, I did the dumbest thing possible and became intensely involved with this man who would never be mine. We fell deeply in love with one another. This love affair was fit for a Shakespearian play. The ghetto version of Romeo and Juliet. The forbidden aspect of our love made it even more passionate. He was deeply conflicted. Torn between the traditionalism of West African culture and the freedom of Western life. He would often say that he wished he never came to America. It was difficult to get a taste of freedom and then go back to bondage. It would have been better to never experience freedom at all.

When he was with me, it was an escape from the life that awaited him. It was an escape from the tradition, the obligations, and the pressure. He was a very serious man who worked very long hours. But with me he was relaxed. He smiled, laughed, danced and was able to experience the unrestricted pleasures that Black American girls so freely give. He would talk about his life and share things that had never left the confines of the left side of his brain. I was his freedom. I was his safe place. I will never forget the day he cried. He said that the happiest moments of his life were when he was with me. My heart was his home. It was my sincere pleasure to be all of this for him. He was so appreciative, and he gave me his heart. He opened up to me. My only mistake was thinking that he would choose me and the life we could have had. I thought he would have the courage to choose the life he wanted and reject the life that had been chosen for him. We argued about this many times. He said it was his destiny. I countered that we choose our destiny. Occasionally, I would ask about her. He would say they were trying to secure her a Visa to come to America. As the months passed, I noticed he was becoming more distant. The times we were together were not as happy as they once were. One day he came over. He sat on the couch for a long time without saying anything. I could tell something was wrong. But, I already knew. She was coming. He told me they secured her Visa and our relationship was over. He told me to move on with my life. I was livid and devastated. I blocked him from my phone and social media and went to tend to my wounds. I was heartbroken. Why didn't he choose the life we could have had? He didn't choose me because he wasn't supposed to. It didn't work out because it wasn't supposed to. I often wondered how a man born more than 5,000 miles away ended up in my life. We were meant to meet, because there was something only he could teach me. There's a quote that says, *"Sometimes a man's purpose in a woman's life is to help her become a better woman...for another man"*. I found closure when I accepted he was never supposed to be mine. He was preparing me for the man that was truly my kindred spirit. Remember in Chapter 1 where I used the quote, "of all the nowheres I've been, you were my favorite". Well, this man was my favorite nowhere.

After that relationship ended, I knew I would never settle for anything less than what I had experienced with that man. I no longer wanted the ring, the wedding or the validation of being in a relationship. I wanted to share my life with someone. I wanted a man to look at me and say, "her heart is my home. She is my safe place from the world, and I can be myself with her. I am safe from racism and societal and familial expectations. I do not have to hide who I am from her. I can express my deepest feelings and emotions. I can give her my heart and know that she will take care of it. I can open up and talk about my past, my failures, my dreams and goals". That man showed me what a sacred relationship was. I felt safe with him. I felt safe to be as soft and vulnerable as I needed to be. He showed me a glimpse of the depths of what a real and lasting love could look like. He wasn't the one. But if a man who wasn't the one could be all of that, imagine what THE ONE would bring.

This has helped me to stay f**k Boy free. I started to look at men to see if there was any depth to him. Is he looking for a heart to call home, or just someone to have sex with? Is he looking for a ride or die life partner to experience all the ups and downs of life with, or is he lost and looking for a place to spend the night? I will tell a man, if you are not willing to give me all of you, then I am not the one. Ladies, we are the essence of all. We embody and encompass everything that a man needs and wants. We are the source of his strength. Don't just give him sex. Give him understanding, patience, unconditional love, and encouragement. Affirm him when the world tears him down. Speak life into him. When he makes mistakes, offer him mercy. Then yell at him later. Tell him how much you adore him and how proud you are of him. Understand that he has been through things just like you. He may have childhood trauma that he is working through. He may have things from his past that still bother him. Give him a listening ear. Don't be so quick to always talk about your problems and off load on him. Often, we view men as our knights in shining armor and in many cases they are. How nice would it be to save him occasionally? Be his friend and confidant. Be more than a pretty face. Have more to offer than pussy. These types of relationships are the ones that last. These types of bonds are unbreakable. F**k boys can't fathom going this deep with a woman. They are not emotionally mature to handle this type of spiritual exchange. But a masculine man can. In fact, this is what he is looking for. This is one of his deepest desires. A favorite quote of mine is, *"share your hell with a good woman and she will show you a way out"*. A f**k boy will run from that proposition. A masculine man will reply, "only if you give me your hell too". Accept that your heart is a home and watch a masculine come knock your door down.

> **Exercise***: If your desire is to be in a relationship or be married, write down the reasons you want to be in a relationship or be married. See if those reasons line up with what a sacred relationship looks like. Choose a couple that you admire and study the ways in which their relationship is based.*

# CHAPTER 10

# Live in Love, not Fear

*"But dear, there is sun after rain, love after pain"*

*Ventum*

\* \* \*

*"Sometimes you have to choose health, life and love over and over again until your being is ready to accept the new version of you"*

*Yung pueblo*

Even today, I'm scared. I've been with my kindred spirit for two years. I fear he may leave. I fear that one day he will wake up and see all my flaws, my imperfections and walk away. Although he's never given me any real reason to doubt him and he's told me countless times he's not going anywhere, my past relationships still linger from time to time. I remember the cheating, the abuse, the lies, the humiliation and the heartbreak, and I think what if it happens again. What if I give my all and I end up alone; again. What if I have to pick up the pieces of my heart yet again. My fears are valid. My ego, which seeks to protect me from further harm reminds me of all that could go wrong. Looking back over my life, my ego might be right. But my higher self is always reminding me that if I live in fear, I will never win. My higher- self reminds me that if I focus on my fears, that is what I will manifest, and I must only focus on my desires. If I live in fear, I will never embrace the fact that there is a man who loves me, accepts me and has decided to make my heart his home. It is a daily decision to live in love instead of fear. I must release the past. I must forgive myself for settling for f**K boys and not loving myself enough to know I deserve better.

I revisit my past as much as I need to. The parts that I cannot let go, I simply let them be. I remind myself that I am deserving of the most wonderful love that exists, and the more I love myself and give myself, the more love will come to me. I recently had a spiritual reading done and the reader asked me, "Are you in a relationship" I said yes, and I said to myself "ok, here we go". She explained, "Your partner holds you in very high regard. He sees you as very beautiful, powerful and strong. But you are not giving him the same energy he is giving you. You are coming off as needy. What you are asking of him, you need to give yourself first". She was right. The way he sees me, I often do not see myself. I still see myself as the woman who was abandoned, who was not chosen, who was lied to, cheated on and left broken. There are times I still see myself as the scared little girl who was violated. It's easy to choose a f**k Boy when you live in fear. But to live in love requires a level of courage that many of us simply are hesitant to adopt. I'm reminded of the saying, *"but what if I fall, oh, but my darling, what if you fly"*. We are so focused on the possibility of falling that we don't even consider the possibility that we may fly! We are so focused on the possibility that every man is the same, or we will end up broken and alone, that we never consider that maybe, just maybe there is a man who considers us to be his greatest blessing. Being f**k Boy free means choosing love over fear every single day. Being f**k Boy free means choosing a future of love and happiness over the repeated past of pain and disappointment. Choosing love over fear takes practice. Our egos, seeking to protect us from future pain tells us to build walls and become jaded. Our egos tell us to not smile and put on extra layers of physical weight as protection. We don't smile and we retreat in our shells. We work long hours, decide to get another degree, another pet, or go on another trip. Anything to protect us from the possibility of another heartbreak. We say there's no good men out there to convince ourselves to not give love another try. But love is beckoning you to tell your ego, thank you for trying to protect me from pain, but I'm going to be ok. The universe loves a woman who takes a chance on herself. The universe supports her and surrounds her with love and boundless opportunities. Kirk Franklin has a song that I love called "Hello Fear". In this song, he is having a conversation with fear explaining that it is time to go their separate ways. The song goes:

*Hello fear*
*I knew I would see you,*
*you have a hard time letting go*
*see these tears,*
*take a good look cause soon they won't fall anymore*
*God's healing my hurtful places*
*That seat that was yours now is taken*
*I'm no longer afraid, see I'm better this way*
*And one more thing before you leave*
*Never again will I love you*
*My heart it refuses to be your home*
*No longer your prisoner*
*Today I remember*
*Apart from you is where I belong*
*And never again will I trust you*
*I'm tired of fighting its been way too long*
*No longer your prisoner*
*Today I remember*
*Who I was*

So yes, even today I have my fears; what if he leaves, what if he finds someone better, what if it doesn't end like I hoped, what if, what if, what if. But then love says, what if he stays, what if you are everything he ever dreamed of, what if this is the happy ending you have dreamed of your whole life. What if, what if, what if...

We must choose love. Even though it may be the hardest thing to do. Even in the midst of our fear, we must always choose love. Start over. Today is a new day. Look forward to what may come instead of what has been. There is freedom in love. You must love yourself enough to take a risk. Trust yourself. You cannot fail. Love is on your side.

> **Exercise:** Take a single piece of paper and divide it in half (either folded or with a pen). On the left side, write down your three greatest fears when it comes to relationships. On the right side, write down an affirmation that combats the fear you have written on the left. For example, a fear could be that you will be abandoned. Being abandoned is rooted in a feeling of unworthiness. On the right, your affirmation will be "I have undeniable worth". Then cut the paper in half, dividing the fears and the positive affirmations. Take the fear side and say out loud "I release these fears as they no longer serve me". Burn up that sheet or flush them down the toilet. Use your 3 positive affirmations to replace those fears and say them daily.

# EPILOGUE

*"I am blooming from the wound where I once bled"*

*Rune Lazuli*

I am grateful for every f**k boy I have met on my journey. Each one entered my life for a reason. It was only after I began healing from the pain of my past that I was able to see them in this light. But there is one man I am not so sure about. I often lament ever having crossed paths with him and the thought of him still stings. Seventeen years later. I didn't speak about him in this book. But I talk about him in my book, When Heartbreak Feels Like Home: Life Lessons in Healing, Loving and Letting Go. He caused the most pain and hurt I have ever experienced. After nearly a decade of no communication, he recently complimented one of my pictures on social media. When I saw that comment, I was instantly triggered, and I went spiraling down memory lane. I called my kindred spirit and he gave me one of his infamous pep talks. He talked about distractions, progress, karma, etc. But the one thing he said that nearly brought me to tears was, "If you never met him, it is possible we never would have met". The fact that he attributed the worst relationship of my life as a catalyst to experience the best relationship of my life was genius. I immediately thought of the quote by Marianne Williamson, *"Having love and lost, I now love more passionately. Having won and lost, I now win more soberly. Having tasted the bitter, I now savor the sweet".* This is what being f**k boy free means to me.

Implementing these 10 strategies has forever changed my life. Learning to let the men from my past go and fully embrace my feminine essence while exerting massive amounts of feminine energy in my daily life has allowed me to tap into my true power as a woman. Using wisdom to exert masculine energy to propel myself to action to become the woman of my dreams has allowed me to love myself in ways I never thought possible. Knowing that I can only be responsible for myself and understanding that I cannot change a man has given me the courage to never settle and walk away if I need to. Embracing that fact that my heart is a home and choosing love over fear daily has caused me to reap enormous benefits. It hasn't been easy, but it has been more than worth it. I hope you too will use these strategies to become f\*\*k boy free!

* * *

*"There's a man somewhere, fighting through life who will one day do anything to call you his everything"*

*S.McNutt*

• • •